Dear Parent:

Congratulations! Your child is taking the first steps on an exciting journey. The destination? Independent reading!

STEP INTO READING® will help your child get there. The program offers five steps to reading success. Each step includes fun stories and colorful art. There are also Step into Reading Sticker Books, Step into Reading Math Readers, Step into Reading Phonics Readers, Step into Reading Write-In Readers, and Step into Reading Phonics Boxed Sets—a complete literacy program with something for every child.

Learning to Read, Step by Step!

Ready to Read   Preschool–Kindergarten
• big type and easy words • rhyme and rhythm • picture clues
For children who know the alphabet and are eager to begin reading.

Reading with Help   Preschool–Grade 1
• basic vocabulary • short sentences • simple stories
For children who recognize familiar words and sound out new words with help.

Reading on Your Own   Grades 1–3
• engaging characters • easy-to-follow plots • popular topics
For children who are ready to read on their own.

Reading Paragraphs   Grades 2–3
• challenging vocabulary • short paragraphs • exciting stories
For newly independent readers who read simple sentences with confidence.

Ready for Chapters   Grades 2–4
• chapters • longer paragraphs • full-color art
For children who want to take the plunge into chapter books but still like colorful pictures.

STEP INTO READING® is designed to give every child a successful reading experience. The grade levels are only guides. Children can progress through the steps at their own speed, developing confidence in their reading, no matter what their grade.

Remember, a lifetime love of reading starts with a single step!

For Melanie Pearce and Adina Solomon,
true friends
—J.K.

For my dear cousin Razel, who, as a
teenager, escaped from the Warsaw ghetto.
And for the ones who didn't.
—E.S.

Special thanks to Phillip J. Ammonds, Anne Frank Center USA, for his time and expertise.
Photograph on p. 48 copyright © AP Photo/Peter Dejong
Additional resources for young readers interested in Anne Frank:
Anne Frank: The Book, the Life, the Afterlife by Francine Prose.
Anne Frank: The Diary of a Young Girl; The Definitive Edition, edited by Otto H. Frank and
   Mirjam Pressler, translated by Susan Massotty.
Anne Frank: Her Life in Words and Pictures by Menno Metselaar and Ruud van der Rol,
   translated by Arnold J. Pomerans. From the archives of the Anne Frank House.

Visit us on the Web!
StepIntoReading.com
randomhouse.com/kids

Educators and librarians, for a variety of teaching tools, visit us at
RHTeachersLibrarians.com

Library of Congress Cataloging-in-Publication Data
Kohuth, Jane.
Anne Frank's chestnut tree / by Jane Kohuth ; illustrated by Elizabeth Sayles.
   p. cm.
ISBN 978-0-449-81255-6 (hardcover) — ISBN 978-0-307-97579-9 (trade pbk.) —
ISBN 978-0-375-97115-0 (lib. bdg.) — ISBN 978-0-375-98113-5 (ebook)
1. Frank, Anne, 1929–1945—Juvenile literature. 2. Jews—Netherlands—Amsterdam—
Biography—Juvenile literature. 3. Jewish children in the Holocaust—Netherlands—Amsterdam—
Juvenile literature. 4. Amsterdam (Netherlands)—Biography—Juvenile literature.
I. Sayles, Elizabeth. II. Title.
DS135.N6F733765 2013 940.53'18092—dc23 [B] 2012034585

Printed in the United States of America
10 9 8 7 6 5 4 3 2 1

STEP INTO READING®   STEP 3

Anne Frank's Chestnut Tree

by Jane Kohuth

illustrated by Elizabeth Sayles

Random House 🏠 New York

In the Attic

It was February 23, 1944.

In the city of Amsterdam,

in an attic at the top

of a tall, narrow building,

a girl sat on the dusty floor.

Through the window
she could see blue sky.
She could see the
bare branches of a chestnut tree.

The tree sparkled with dew.

"As long as this exists,"

the girl thought,

"this sunshine and

this cloudless sky,

and as long as I can enjoy it,

how can I be sad?"

The girl's name was Anne Frank.

She had not been outside

for 597 days.

The Secret Annex

Once, Anne lived a normal life.
She collected
pictures of movie stars.
She read and wrote
and acted in plays.
She liked to make people laugh.

Anne did well in school.

She talked a lot in class.

Anne was always full of thoughts
and opinions.

She had many friends.

She had a happy life.

But on May 10, 1940,

Anne's world changed.

World War II reached her home.

Germany invaded Holland,

the tiny country where Anne lived.

The Nazi Party,

led by Adolf Hitler,

ruled Germany.

The Nazis blamed the world's

problems on Jewish people,

even though they were

a small minority.

Anne and her family were Jewish.

The Nazis made laws against
Jewish people.
Anne had to change schools.
She couldn't go swimming
or see the movies she loved.
Anne's family had to sew
yellow stars on their clothes.
All because they were Jewish.

In July 1942, a letter came for
Anne's older sister, Margot.
The Nazis wanted to send her
to a concentration camp.

Anne's parents knew that
when Jews were sent away,
they were never heard from again.
They had a plan.
The family would hide.

Anne packed her schoolbag.
First she packed the diary
she'd gotten for her
thirteenth birthday.

She stuffed in books,

hair curlers, and letters.

Later she wrote,

"I stuck the craziest things

in the bag, but I'm not sorry.

Memories mean more to me

than dresses."

Early the next morning,
Anne got dressed.
She put on layers of clothing
even though it was summer.

She didn't get to say goodbye
to anyone but her cat.
The family left the
breakfast dishes on the table.
Then they rushed away.

The hiding place

had four small rooms.

They were tucked away

behind a bookcase

above Anne's father's office.

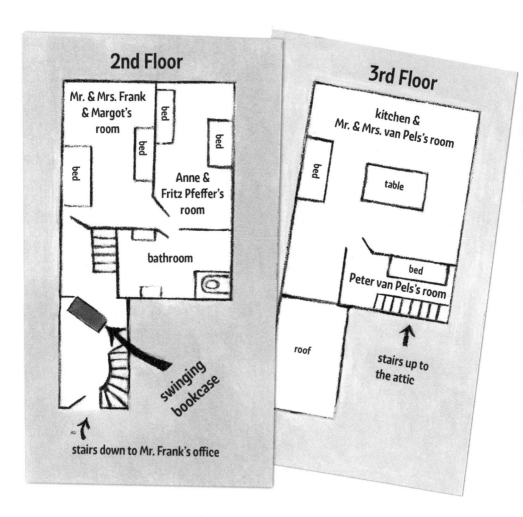

2nd Floor

Mr. & Mrs. Frank
& Margot's
room

bed

bed

bed

bed

Anne &
Fritz Pfeffer's
room

bathroom

swinging
bookcase

stairs down to Mr. Frank's office

3rd Floor

kitchen &
Mr. & Mrs. van Pels's room

bed

table

bed

Peter van Pels's room

roof

stairs up to
the attic

From a window in her new room,

Anne could see a chestnut tree.

But then the windows

had to be covered.

If anyone saw Anne's family,

they might be arrested.

Anne called the hiding place
the Secret Annex.
At first it felt like an adventure.
But as time went on,
life became harder.
Four more people moved in.
Anne had to share a room
with a dentist.

There was little food.

They had to be very quiet.

At night they listened

to the radio,

hoping the war would be over.

Only a few people knew

where Anne's family was.

These helpers brought food,

clothes, and other supplies.

If they were caught,

they would be arrested.

But the helpers never complained.

Anne and the other children
did schoolwork every day.
Anne loved when their helpers
brought books and news.
But she still missed home.
Writing helped Anne feel better.

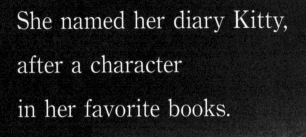

She named her diary Kitty,
after a character
in her favorite books.

Anne told Kitty her fears

for her friends outside.

She told Kitty about the planes

that dropped bombs at night.

Guns on the ground

fired at the planes.

The Secret Annex shook.

Anne climbed into bed
with her parents,
but she was still afraid.

When Anne was very scared,

she ran up and down,

up and down the stairs.

She told Kitty she felt

like a bird trapped in a cage.

"Let me out,

where there's fresh air

and laughter!" she wrote.

In the world around her,

Anne saw fighting and fear.

But in the blue sky above,

she saw beauty and peace.

So she climbed up to the attic.

The windows there

were not covered.

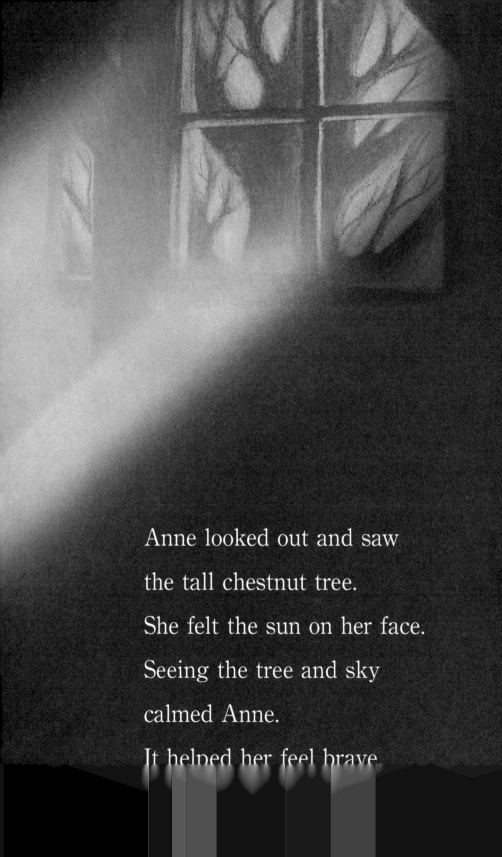

Anne looked out and saw
the tall chestnut tree.
She felt the sun on her face.
Seeing the tree and sky
calmed Anne.
It helped her feel brave.

Anne stayed up late to glimpse
the moon from a window.

She noticed the passing seasons
by watching the chestnut tree
grow buds and leaves.

Anne put nature into her stories.
In a story called "Fear,"
a girl flees a city
where bombs are falling.
She reaches a meadow.
She lies down in the grass.
She looks at the moon and stars
and realizes she's not
afraid anymore.

Nature made Anne feel
that God had not left her.
She wrote in her diary,
"I firmly believe that nature can
bring comfort to all who suffer."

Anne decided she wanted
to be a writer.
Maybe her words would mean
something to other people.
She worked for weeks
editing her diary.
She was almost done.

But on August 4, 1944,

the police found the Secret Annex.

The Nazis sent Anne's family

and two of their helpers

to concentration camps.

Anne's Chestnut Tree

Anne did not survive the war.

But her diary did.

After the Franks were taken away,

helpers crept back to the Annex.

A helper named Miep Gies

hid the pages in her desk.

She saved Anne's writing.

Millions of people

have read Anne's words.

Anne wrote,

"I want to go on living

even after my death!"

She has.

Today you can visit
Anne's Secret Annex.
You can peer up the stairs
into the attic.
You can see where Anne
gazed at the sky
and the great chestnut tree.

Visitors loved the tree.

For them it stood for hope.

When the tree became sick,

people tried to save it.

They braced the tree to hold it up.

But in 2010,

a storm knocked it down.

Even so, Anne's tree lives on.
People grew saplings
from the tree's chestnuts.
Hundreds were planted in
Amsterdam.
Others were planted at schools
named for Anne around the world.
In the United States,
saplings will grow in important
places across the country.

Like the saplings
from her chestnut tree,
Anne Frank's words have been
planted around the world.
They have been planted
in schools, museums,
and libraries.
They have been planted
in the minds of the millions
who read her diary.
And there they grow,
inspiring people to see the world
as Anne did.

*"When I look up at the sky, I somehow feel
that everything will change for the better,
that this cruelty too will end, that peace and
tranquility will return once more."*
—*Anne Frank (1929–1945)*

History is not just dates and places. History is people. It's children like you, speaking to us. Anne Frank's voice comes to us from a terrible time, out of a terrible place. It's a gift that shows us that you can keep trying to be a good person, even when so many people have decided to do evil.

To learn more about Anne and the time she lived in, visit the Anne Frank House online at AnneFrank.org.